Verse and Worse

You are holding a reproduction of an original work that is in the public domain in the United States of America, and possibly other countries. You may freely copy and distribute this work as no entity (individual or corporate) has a copyright on the body of the work. This book may contain prior copyright references, and library stamps (as most of these works were scanned from library copies). These have been scanned and retained as part of the historical artifact.

This book may have occasional imperfections such as missing or blurred pages, poor pictures, errant marks, etc. that were either part of the original artifact, or were introduced by the scanning process. We believe this work is culturally important, and despite the imperfections, have elected to bring it back into print as part of our continuing commitment to the preservation of printed works worldwide. We appreciate your understanding of the imperfections in the preservation process, and hope you enjoy this valuable book.

Verse and Worse

LIBRARY of CONGRESS
Two Copies Received
MAR 21 1906
Copyright Entry
Mar 28, 1906
CLASS a XXc. No.
141861
COPY B.

PS 3521
.I63 V4
1906

SELECTED AND ARRANGED
BY
CLARENCE W. KIP
1906

DEDICATED TO

My Mother

VERSE AND WORSE

GATHERED from different places at various times, and herein bound, to please a few select friends.

No claim is made as to the authorship—where the author's name is known, it is given.

The only excuse I have for publishing this book is that I was dared to do so, and I make no apologies.

As I expect to derive a handsome income from the sale of this book, the few who will not clamor for more, after reading it, can do as they see fit about advising others to read it, as the book-sellers and I will not notice such a minute minority.

CLARENCE W. KIP.

VERSE & WORSE

TO MY MOTHER.

Deal gently with her Time; these many years
Of life have brought more smiles with them
    than tears.
Lay not thy hand too harshly on her now,
But trace decline so slowly on her brow
That, (like the sunset of the Northern clime,
Where twilight lingers in the summer time,
And fades at last into the silent night,
E'er one may note the passing of the light),
So may she pass—since 'tis the common lot—
As one who, resting, sleeps, and knows it not.
       J. A. Weyth.

VERSE & WORSE

FLORENCE.
AN ACROSTIC.

Fair minded, just, trustworthy and sensible,
Loving and lovable; with a well defined sense
Of right and wrong.   Above little things,
Reasonably jealous of what you hold dear;
Ever believing in those you consider friends;
Now and then, a little spunky and childlike.
Crowning all, is your womanhood—
Ever the best and noblest trait of my ideal.
Clarence W. Kip.

VERSE & WORSE

I LOVED THEE.

I loved thee for that dear, deep lovingness
    Resting within thy tender brooding eyes;
I loved thee for thy wealth of womanhood,
    Thy quiet questionings, thy sweet replies,
Thy patient brows that knew no bitter mood.
                Geo. Armstrong.

I fear that more men turn monks for the love of woman than for the love of God.

Some day my harvest will be gathered in, small and scant as it is, but I know the Reaper will forgive its pathetic broken store. And in whatever land you dwell I want my face turned towards you, so that if there be dreaming in the dark, I may dream of you.

VERSE & WORSE

LEFT.

"Meet me," she said, "by the orchard wall
Tomorrow night, as the sun goes down."
And this is tomorrow, and here am I,
And there's the wall, and the sun's gone down.

H. G. Chapman.

A woman tells more lies; but a man tells them better.

LACHRYMAE RERUM.

God made woman, form and face
    He shaped with all the skill he knew;
He gave her beauty, wit, and grace,
    But—God forgot to make her true.

Anonymous.

VERSE & WORSE

LOVE SONG.

If death should claim me for her own today,
    And softly I should falter from your side,
Oh, tell me, loved one, would my memory stay,
    And would my image in your heart abide?
Or should I be as some forgotten dream,
    That lives its little space, then fades entire?
Should time send o'er you its relentless stream,
    To cool your heart and quench for aye love's fire?

I would not for the world, love, give you pain,
    Or ever compass what would cause you grief;
And, oh how well I know that tears are vain!
    But love is sweet, my dear, and life is brief;
So if some day before you I should go
    Beyond the sound and sight of song and sea,
'Twould give my spirit stronger wings to know
    That you remembered still and wept for me.

Paul L. Dunbar.

VERSE & WORSE

A MEMORY.

When I kissed you on the stair,
    The perfume
Of the roses in your hair,
Drifted, swooning on the air
    Thro' the gloom;
And your sighs, and your eyes,
    Soft as any dove's,
Whispered you were nearest,
Told me you were dearest
    Of my loves.

When I kissed you on the stair,
    On my heart
Lay a heavy weight of care,
For I knew that then and there
    We must part:
Far away, are you gay?
    And do you forget?
While the witching memory lingers
Of your cool caressing fingers
    With me yet.
              G. W. Carryl.

VERSE & WORSE

CONTENTMENT.

'Tis bliss for me; let all my cares
Betake their sorrows far away,
I know not where! I know not when
My happy heart or tongue can pen
The words which now my heart doth
    say,
" 'Tis bliss to be with thee."
Clarence W. Kip.

No man is good enough to marry a good woman.

One can love once and honorably, with his whole being, but not truly and honorably love a second time, at least not in a manner like unto the first.

VERSE & WORSE

FANCY'S REALM.

What happy forms my fancies weave
   'Mid night's grim hours, dark and still;
The happiness I may achieve—
   Reality lies dead and chill.

I plan for joyous journeys to
   Some distant land where bliss holds sway:
The one I love—I speak of you—
   Beside me happy all the way.

And now I dream of your embrace,
   So strong, so noble and so true.
It seems I look into your face—
   Deep in your eyes your heart I view.

Your lips meet mine—a clinging kiss—
   Till gaunt Death calls 'twill treasured be—
What sacredness I find in this;
   E'en Death can't sever it from me.
                   Clarence W. Kip.

VERSE & WORSE

SILENCE.
'Tis better to sit here beside the sea,
    Here on the spray-kissed beach,
In silence, that between such friends as we
    Is full of deepest speech.
Selected.

God be thanked, the meanest of his creatures boasts two soul-sides—one to face the world with, and one to show a woman, when he loves her.

Woman must keep herself unspotted, yet be content to wed with impurity.

VERSE & WORSE

GHOSTS.

'Tis in the wierd strange stillness of the night
That ghosts creep out!
'Tis then that wrong and right,
Nude, gaunt and spectre-like,
Stand wide apart, and we must choose
If head, or heart, or passion win the day;
And on the soul are wrought
Those wounds which conscience makes
In the dissecting room of thought.

Selected.

I have wondered vainly many times why I love you, and tried to pick out this quality and that for especial regard. This afternoon I found out. It is your crystalline, exquisite honour. The purity of most women is negative; they are clean because they are not otherwise. Yours is positive. You are white because God made you so, and mingled with this is a holy joy in your whiteness.

VERSE & WORSE

THE FIRST KISS.

It took so long to say "good-bye;"
The curtains were half drawn, and I—
For once I seemed to hesitate,
She seemed so pleased to have me wait;
And so we let the minutes fly.

The hours just then were all awry;
" 'Tis early yet," I heard her sigh.
The clock responded "It is late,"
    It took so long.

Now there was no one near to spy
A maiden and her lover shy.
Ah, well! I can't quite demonstrate
Just how her lips met mine.
    'Twas Fate!
Love's first sweet kiss, and that is why
    It took so long.
                    F. Carmen.

    She gave him, not an opportunity, but opportunities to make an opportunity—which is vastly different.

VERSE & WORSE

HIS WIFE.

Somehow I never seem to mind the men—
They look a minute, then they look away—
But it's the women I mind most; they
   Whisper, and lift their eyes, and stare
      again,
And I stare back as if I didn't care—
   Care, while my throat chokes and my eyes
      are dim.
It's not for me, but oh, to think they dare
   To laugh at Jim, my Jim.

   Perhaps I shouldn't mind—I ought to be
Used to their sneers and grins by now, God
      knows,
And yet—how this train stops and backs and
      slows
   And waits for more to look at him and me.
"Only a little glass or two," he said.
   Oh! my poor boy, how gay he looked and
      trim.
I used to think I'd rather see him—dead,
   But oh, its Jim, my Jim.

VERSE & WORSE

HIS WIFE—Continued.

I wonder if those staring women think
I envy them their husbands sitting there
Prim and sedate?   The fools, I rather bear
  With everything, the pain, the shame, the drink,
And be his wife, his wife to help him so;
  His wife to love him and come for him,
How proud I used to be, how proud, and oh,
  To think it's Jim, my Jim.
Theodosia Garrison.

I think the hardest thing a man of the world has to do, when he falls in love with a good true woman, is to convince himself that he is worthy of her love.

VERSE & WORSE

NIGHT.

Slowly night falls the day is done;
The day's work ceases with the sun,

And thro' the night deep slumber brings
Its rest so dear—and dreams on wings.

Naught matters then, 'tis God holds sway,
Guarding us equally night and day;

So when I seek my bed to rest,
He keeps the one I love the best.

Waking, I shield you from all harm,
But Night's grim darkness brings alarm.

Each night your safety is my prayer,
God hears, and keeps you in his care.
Clarence W. Kip.

VERSE & WORSE

DREAMS.

What dreams we have and how they fly
Like rosy clouds across the sky;
Of wealth, of fame, of sure success,
Of love that comes to cheer and bless;
And how they wither, how they fade,
The waning wealth, the jilting jade—
The fame that for a moment gleams,
Then flies forever—dreams, ah—dreams!

O burning doubt and long regret,
O tears with which our eyes are wet,
Heart-throbs, heart-aches, the glut of pain,
The somber cloud, the bitter rain,
You were not of those dreams—ah, well,
Your full fruition who can tell?
Wealth, fame, and love, ah! love that beams
Upon our souls, all dreams—ah! dreams.
Paul L. Dunbar.

It is as hard—to some natures harder—to take good news strongly than to take bad.

VERSE & WORSE

A WALTZ IN DREAMLAND.

I am dancing tonight with demure Isabelle,
    The girl with the jet black hair,
The form of a Goddess, the steps of a queen,
    And a brow serene and fair.

Isabelle has eyes of intensest black,
    And ivory teeth that gleam
Thro' a mouth like a poppy-bud dipped in dew,
    In a smile like a wood-nymph's dream.

And the waltz refrain is a paean of joy
    That hallows the gorgeous knell,
And the violins sing like the slaves of a king,
    As I dance with Isabelle.

I am dancing tonight with Isabelle;
    We glide thro' the glittering hall,
And proud is her pose; sedate her mien—
    She knows she's the belle of the ball.

And her nectar breath is warm on my cheek,
    And her black eyes sparkle and shine;
As I thrill with a passion I dare not speak,
    Her heart pressed close to mine.

VERSE & WORSE

A WALTZ IN DREAMLAND—Continued.

Pulse on, violins, with your tenderest strains,
    Shine, lamps, in your diamond shell,
For my heart is as light as a feather tonight
    As I dance with Isabelle.

There arises a chaos of minor notes
    Like the plaint of a soul for its sins,
And across the hot night like a requiem floats
    The dirge of the violins.

. . . .

And awakening out of this blissful trance
    My senses know and say
I've imagined it all—the lights, the dance—
    Isabelle is miles away!

And the waltz refrain is all shadows and tears,
    And Fancy holds its spell,
For 'tis all in a dream that I dimly seem
    To be dancing with Isabelle.

Anonymous.

VERSE & WORSE

LOVE.

Love is a day
    With no thought of morrow.
Love is a joy
    With no thought of sorrow.
Love is to give
    With no thought of receiving.
Love is to trust
    Without quite believing.
                    Selected.

A man falls in love with a pretty little caterpillar; he wakes up and find himself married to a butterfly.

The dignity of womanhood was never so safe, as when women thus confidently left its guardianship to the instinctive chivalry of men.

VERSE & WORSE

SOUL TORTURE.

Why do I see thy face in everything,
   Whether I ope my tear-stained eyes,
Or drop the fringèd curtain on my orbs?
   Canst thou not wipe away my tears and
      sighs?

Why, when in the fastness of my room
   I sit and read by flickering candle-light,
Why can I not control my mind——or heart,
   Why must I sit and dream of thee all
      night?
                Clarence W. Kip.

   Laughter is often nothing but the froth of tears.

   Without love, each kiss adds to the woman's regard for the man, but takes away from his desire for her.

VERSE & WORSE

"BOHEMIA."

I'd rather live in Bohemia,
Than in any other land,
For only there are values true,
And laurels gathered in all men's view.
Here Pilgrims stream, with a faith sublime,
From every class, and clime, and time,
Aspiring only to be enrolled,
With the names that are writ in the Book of Gold.
And each one bears in mind, or in hand,
The palm of his dear Bohemia land.
The scholar first with his book, the youth
Aflame with the glory of harvested truth,
A girl with a picture, a man with a play,
A boy with a wolf he has modeled in clay.
The smith, with his marvelous hilt and sword,
A player, a king, a plowman, a lord.
And the player is king when the door is passed,
The plowman is crowned, and the lord is last.

Oh I'd rather fail in Bohemia,
Than win in another land.
There are no titles inherited there,
No horde nor hope for the brainless heir.

VERSE & WORSE

"BOHEMIA."—Continued.

No gilded dullard native born,
To gaze on his fellow with leaden scorn.
Bohemia has none but adopted sons;
Its limits where fancy's bright stream runs,
Her honors not garnered for thrift nor trade,
But for beauty and truth that men's souls
    were made.
To the empty heart in a jeweled breast,
There is value perhaps in a purchased crest;
But the thirsty of soul soon learn to know
The moistureless froth of the social show,
The vulgar sham of the pompous feast,
Where the heaviest purse is highest priest;
The organized charity, scrimped and iced,
In the name of a cautious, statistical Christ;
The smile restrained, the respectful cant,
For a friend indeed is a friend in want.
Where the only aim is to keep afloat,
And a brother may drown with a cry in his
    throat.
Oh I sigh for the glow of a kindly heart,
And the grasp of a friendly hand,
And I'd rather live in Bohemia,
Than in any other land.
                    R. J. C.

VERSE & WORSE

HEART SACRIFICE.

If I had loved him less, perhaps,
   I do not know—one cannot know—
He might have loved me more, and I
   Should not have felt within me grow
The crying loneliness which comes
   To women's hearts that love and wait
In longing, hopeless hopefulness
   Outside the unpermitting gate.

And yet, if I had loved him less,
   I should not know—one could not know—
The rapture of love's sacrifice.
   Those fires, through ashes, always glow
To light the long, hard way that leads
   The faltering spirit up to see
The infinite unselfishness
   Which saved mankind on Calvary.
              Wm. J. Lampton.

   The world is cumbered with the wreck of lives which, but for the lack of love, would have been great.

VERSE & WORSE

SELECTION.

Ah, Love! could you and I with Him conspire
To grasp this sorry scheme of things entire,
Would not we shatter it to bits—and then
Remold it nearer to the heart's desire?
   Rubaiyat of Omar Khayyam.

A fool can win the love of a man, but it requires a woman of resources to keep it.

In a maiden's words no one should place faith, nor in what a woman says; for on a turning wheel have their hearts been formed, and guile in their breasts been laid.

VERSE & WORSE

NEED A BODY CRY.

All girls must kiss and smile or frown
   And be in love, because
The stern decree is written down
   In Nature's changeless laws.
So here is to the pretty maid
   Who lets her lips meet mine,
And frankly owns she's not afraid
   To give Love's countersign.

Ho! Ho! Ho! Ho! I think no less
Of her who brings me bliss,
   Because I know
   She trusts me so;
I know whom she will kiss.

Here's to the maid as cold as ice
   The maid of modesty,
Who says that "kissing isn't nice,"
   Which means she won't kiss me.
She kisses someone—that is clear,
   There's someone else who can
Approach her lips with little fear,
   But I am not the man.

VERSE & WORSE

NEED A BODY CRY—Continued.

Ho! Ho! Ho! Ho! the maid of ice!
The coy and prim young miss.
   Without a sigh
   I pass her by
And think, "Whom does she kiss?"
                 H. Romaine.

It would be a peaceful world if we could only realize that the fever of love is like other fevers. It comes to a crisis and the patient either dies or is cured. It cannot last at the same point forever.

A man must love some woman, but ofttimes the question of whom he shall love seems to be at the mercy of accident.

VERSE & WORSE

TO A FRIEND.

Marvel not I seek the friendship
Of one whose soul enjoys the music
Of poetry. And whose charms meet
With her as strangers, while they too quick
Ensnare me to a fate so sweet.

Clarence W. Kip.

Friendship is never complete until it is tried in the fire of sorrow.

Seize Love at whatever age he comes to you—if you can avoid being ridiculous.

VERSE & WORSE

A GENOESE LOVE SONG.

I've told you many times, O, Rosalia,
    That you're my life, my love, my rose of May;
But deaf to all my prayers, you idly hear,
    Then with a little laugh you skip away.
'Tis not a world I ask for, Rosalia,
    Only just a look, a word, a kiss;
One little kiss—'twould cost you nothing, dear,
    Your sweet mouth keeps too many one to miss.
Only just one! and then 'twill all be over;
    I'll go and die!—I shall not care for life:
At least—unless you'll let me be your lover,
    And marry me, and be my little wife.

Anonymous.

Wit is needful to him who travels far; at home all is easy.

VERSE & WORSE

A PRAYER.

A morrow must come on
  When I shall wake to weep;
But just for some short hours,
  God, give me sleep!

I ask not hope's return.
  As I have sowed, I reap.
Grief must awake with dawn;
  Yet, oh, to sleep.

No dreams, dear God, no dreams,
  Mere slumber, dull and deep,
Such as Thou givest brutes,—
  Sleep, only sleep!
                    Selected.

And if the cup you drink, the lip you press,
Ends in what all begins and ends in "Yes."
Imagine then you are what heretofore
You were—hereafter you shall not be less.

VERSE & WORSE

DO YOU REMEMBER?

Do you remember when you heard
My lips breathe Love's first faltering word?
    You do, sweet, don't you,
When having wandered all the day,
Linked arm in arm, I dared to say,
    You'll love me—won't you?
And when you blushed and could not speak,
I fondly kissed your glowing cheek;
    Did that affront you?
Oh, surely not; your eye exprest
No wrath, but said, perhaps in jest,
    You'll love me, won't you?
I'm sure my eyes replied, "I will;"
And you believe that promise still;
    You do, sweet, don't you?
Yes, yes, when age has made our eyes
Unfit for questions or replies,
    You'll love me, won't you?

Thos. Bagley.

VERSE & WORSE

TO ONE I KNOW.

Plain, frank and earnest, indeed, with a wealth of womanhood hid 'neath the surface.

Yes, one who inspires a sense of submission to strength.

Not an idle power to worship in vain.

But the regal throne of a queen, who unconsciously wields her omnipresent charms to the benefit of her acquaintances.

Clarence W. Kip.

VERSE & WORSE

THE TRAVELLER.

Who travels alone with his eyes on the heights
Tho' he laugh in the daytime oft weeps in
 the nights.
For courage goes down at the set of the sun,
When the toil of the journey is all borne by
 one.
He speeds but to grief tho' full gayly he ride,
Who travels alone without Love at his side.

Who travels alone without lover or friend,
But hurries from nothing to naught at the end,
Tho' great be his winnings and high be his goal,
He is bankrupt in wisdom and beggared in soul.
Life's one gift of value to him is denied,
Who travels alone without Love at his side.

It is easy enough in this world to make haste,
If one live for that purpose—but think of the
 waste!
For life is a poem to leisurely read
And the joy of the journey lies not in the
 speed,
Oh, vain the achievement and petty his pride,
Who travels alone without Love at his side.

Ella W. Wilcox.

VERSE & WORSE

THE DEBUTANTE.

Here in her dainty chamber,
   In the snow-white bed it lies,
The dress that brought such a sparkle
   Of joy to her violet eyes.

A wonderful garment fashioned
   In yards upon yards of lace,
With knots of silvery ribbon
   To fasten the folds in place.

So, lay it away forever
   In the sweet dead leaves of the rose,
With the fan, and the fairy slippers,
   The gloves and the silken hose.

The bodice too, that was fitted
   To her girlish and graceful shape,
And heavy with frosty fringes
   The long white opera cape.

VERSE & WORSE

THE DEBUTANTE—Continued.

For Madge—she is done with dancing,
    And the pleasures and pains of life—
No babe shall call her "Mother"—
    No man shall call her "Wife."

For below in the darkened parlour,
    With her slender feet unshod,
She lies on a couch of lilies
    All dressed for the Court of God.
Selected.

A TOAST!

Here's to a true woman—God's masterpiece.

VERSE & WORSE

REGRET.

I sometimes think, beloved, had we not met,
You might have had a fuller life; and yet
It is not given us, dear, to forget.
I cannot put away from out my life
Its one sustaining comfort. Ah, the strife
Is hard and bitter, darling, and the knife
That wounds us both was forged by mine
       own hand—
Cruel before you I must ever stand.
Anonymous.

It is so inconvenient to be a widow, because it is necessary to resume the modesty of a young girl, without being able to feign her ignorance.

Any possible move is a probable move, provided it is in the wrong direction.

VERSE & WORSE

LOVE'S MURDERER.

Since Love is dead—stretched here between
    us, dead,
Let us be sorry for the quiet clay;
Hope and offense alike have passed away.
The glory long had left his vanquished head,
Poor shadowed glory of a distant day!
But can you give no pity in its stead?
I see your hard eyes have no tears to shed,
But has your heart no kindly word to say?

Were you his murderer, or was I?
I do not care to ask, there is no need
Since gone is gone, and dead is dead indeed,
What use to wrangle of the how, and why?
I take all blame, I take it, draw not nigh!
Ah, do not touch him, lest Love's corpse
    should bleed.
Selected.

    The friend with whom one does not have to make explanations is God-given.

VERSE & WORSE

NO WONDER.

"No wonder me darlin' is cross-eyed,"
   Said love-sick young Pat to his mother,
"For both of her eyes are so pretty,
   That each wants to look at the other."
               F. F. Easton.

Marrying is like furnishing—there's room for taste if you have time.

A man is as good as he has to be—a woman as bad as she dares.

There's a whole lot of difference between a great man of wealth, and a man of great wealth. Them last is getting terrible common.

VERSE & WORSE

SONG.

Your kiss beloved was to me
As if all the flowers of Araby,
And every fresh and fragrant rose
That ever blew, shall blow, or blows,
Had all her sweetness taken up
And poured into one perfect cup
For me to drain—
Kiss me again!
Governeur Morris.

A picket frozen on duty,
   A mother starved for her brood,
Socrates drinking his hemlock,
   And Jesus on the rood;
The millions, who, humble and nameless,
   The straight hard pathway trod—
Some call it Consecration,
   And others call it God.
Anonymous.

VERSE & WORSE

IMMORTALITY.

Two caterpillars crawling on a leaf
By some strange accident in contact came;
Their conversation, passing all belief,
Was that same argument, the very same,
That has been "proed and conned" from man
      to man,
Yea, ever since this wondrous world began.
The ugly creatures, deaf and dumb and blind,
Devoid of features that adorn mankind,
Were vain enough in dull and wordy strife
To speculate upon a future life.
The first was optimistic, full of hope;
The second, quite dyspeptic, seemed to mope.
Said number one, "I'm sure of our salvation."
Said number two, "I'm sure of our damnation;
Our ugly forms alone would seal our fates
And bar our entrance through the pearly
      gates.
Suppose that death should take us unawares,
How could we climb the golden stairs?
If maidens shun us as they pass us by,
Would angels bid us welcome in the sky?

IMMORTALITY—Continued.

I wonder what great crimes we have com-
    mitted
That leave us so forlorn and so unpitied?
Perhaps we've been ungrateful, unforgiving;
'Tis plain to me that life's not worth the
    living."
"Come, come, cheer up," the jovial worm
    replied,
"Let's take a look upon the other side;
Suppose we cannot fly like moths or millers,
Are we to blame for being caterpillars?
Will that same God that doomed us crawl the
    earth
A prey to every bird that's given birth,
Forgive our captor as he eats and sings
And damn poor us, because we have not
    wings?
If we can't skim the air like owl or bat,
A worm will turn 'for a' that,' "
They argued thro' the summer, autumn nigh,
The ugly things composed themselves to die;
And so, to make their funeral quite complete,
Each wrapped him in his little winding sheet.
The tangled web encompassed them full soon,
Each made him for his coffin a cocoon;

VERSE & WORSE

IMMORTALITY—Continued.

All thro' the winter's chilling blast they lay,
Dead to the world, aye, dead as human clay.
Lo, spring comes forth with all her warmth
    and love;
She brings sweet justice from the realms above
She brings the Chrysalis, she resurrects the
    dead;
Two butterflies ascend encircling her head,
And so this emblem shall forever be
A sign of immortality.
                    Joseph Jefferson.

Here's to the Garden of Eden
Which Adam was always a-weedin';
   Till Eve by mistake
   Got bit by a snake
Who on the ripe pippins was feedin'!

Then a longing it seemed to possess her
For clothing sufficient to dress her;
   And ever since then
   It's been up to us men
To pay for her dresses—God bless her!
                    Anonymous.

VERSE & WORSE

A MAIDEN TO HER MIRROR.

He said he loved me. Then he called my
    hair
Silk threads wherewith sly Cupid strings his
    bow,
My cheeks a rose leaf fallen on new snow;
And swore my round full throat would bring
    despair
To Venus or Psyche.
        Time and care
Will fade these locks; the merry God, I trow,
Uses no grizzled cords upon his bow.
How will it be when I, no longer fair,
Plead for his kiss with cheeks whence long
    ago
The early snow-flake melted quite away,
The rose leaf died—and in whose sallow
    clay
Lie the deep sunken tracks of Life's gaunt
    crow?
When this full throat shall wattle fold on fold,
Like some ripe peach left dying on the wall,
Or like a spent accordion, when all
The music has exhaled—will love grow cold?
              Ella W. Wilcox.

VERSE & WORSE

AUF WIEDERSEHEN.

In the brown of her eyes
A soft light lies,
  The light of her upturned face;
The slow retreat
Of the cadence sweet,
  With the roses and ribbons and lace—
The soft refrain,
The dying strain—
  The waltz is our last,—
      "Auf wiedersehen."
H. S. Candee.

The good God had to compromise with the first woman he created almost at once, and men have done it ever since, and have never had the best of it.

VERSE & WORSE

HAD WE NOT MET.

Had we not met—Fate changed her plans,
   What would your life have missed and lost
Of joy and satisfying fullness?
   Do not count the cost
         To me.

Had we not met: I'd not have gained
   The power to ask, and beg, and plead
Repeatedly for that which you withhold
   As often as I tell my need
         To thee.

But we have met! You need not fear,
   For dear one, when you go,
You'll drop me from your life
   Without a trace—as sun melts snow.

Do you deny it? Well, I'll say,
   Perhaps I've helped you pass some
Weary day or night less wearily—
   But still your kisses never come
         To me.
              Clarence W. Kip.

VERSE & WORSE

A CHORD.

I love you, dear. When I have said the words,
  My lips grow dumb, speech has been beggared quite,
As if some mastering hand had swept the chords
  Of all my life into one chord of might,
That rang—and snapt! . . . And I, the quivering lute,
Throbbing with music still, must evermore be mute!
The Century.

I have often wondered why Providence should have been so sparing of metal when making a woman's heart; enough went into her tongue to give it a keen edge; but her heart—no steel or flint or sand; just a soft little pudgy mud-pie that any man can dent with his fingers.

VERSE & WORSE

TO AN UNKNOWN GODDESS.

I can picture fair Venus on her throne;
Her many suitors longing for a nod. Yes,
Willing to die but for a glance;
And you are my Goddess.
And I too glad to do thy will—
Thou canst say "Slave, go," or "Slave, be still,"
And my speed, quickened by some unknown power,
Bears me along to do thy beloved command:
And back I come, a joyous, happy slave,
Thrilled thro' and thro' to be at thy right hand.

Clarence W. Kip.

To his friend a man should be a friend,—to him and to his friend; but no man should be the friend of his foe's friend.

VERSE & WORSE

TO AN ASTROLOGER.

Nay, seer, I do not doubt thy mystic lore,
Nor question that the tenor of my life,
Past, present, and future, is revealed
There in my horoscope.   I do believe
That yon dead moon compels the haughty seas
To ebb and flow, and that my natal star
Stands like a stern-browed sentinel in space
And challenges events; nor lets one grief,
Or joy, or failure, or success pass on
To mar or bless my earthly lot, until
It proves its Karmic right to come to me.
All this I grant, but more than this I know!
Before the solar systems were conceived,
When nothing was but the unnamable,
My spirit lived, an atom of the cause.
Thro' countless ages, and in many forms
It has existed, ere it entered in
This human frame to serve its little day
Upon the earth.   The Deathless me of me,
The spark from that all-creative fire
Is part of that eternal source called God,
And mightier than the universe.

VERSE & WORSE

TO AN ASTROLOGER—Continued.

                        Why he
Who knows, and knowing, never once forgets
The pedigree divine of his own soul,
Can conquer, shape, and govern destiny
And use vast space as 'twere a board for
       chess
With stars for pawns; can change his horo-
       scope
To suit his will; turn failure to success,
And from preordained sorrows harvest joy.
There is no puny planet, sun or moon,
Or zodiacal sign which can control
The God in us!
If we bring that to bear
Upon events, we mould them to our wish;
'Tis when the infinite 'neath the finite gropes
That men are governed by their horoscopes.
                 Ella W. Wilcox.

    It is only through suffering that we grow, and when we suffer enough, we are great.

VERSE & WORSE

SONG.

All the stars in Heaven shine brighter,
    Love, for love of you.
All the fleecy clouds are whiter,
    Love, for love of you.
And my heart, before so downcast, now is
        lighter.

Every violet is bluer,
    Love, for love of you.
Every bird note ringeth truer,
    Love, for love of you.
And my heart is quickened, stronger, better,
        newer.
                      Selected.

    It is a strange decree of Fate that when a man loves a woman, he must give up everything he has of hers, if she cannot give him all.

VERSE & WORSE

SOLACE.

I strove to bury sorrow in a crowd,
    And feared to sit with memory apart—
The world, I thought, should tutor us to feel
    How light a thing it is to break one's heart.

But when I left the laughing, jesting throng,
    Weary, embittered by the loneliness,
And sought the firelit silence—lo, Dear Heart,
    Remembrance cheered me with your own caress!

Joan Burleigh.

There is an element of mother-love in the devotion which some women give to men.

Most women love Love, not the lover.

VERSE & WORSE

MY CONFESSION.

I cannot tell just how, or why I feel
   Quite as I do   But this I know—
   Within the twilight's beauty all aglow,
Before your altar white, I'd like to kneel,

And tell you of my fondest hopes and fears,
   My aims in life, my failures and defeats,
   And how, sometimes, my life with victory meets,
Until your eyelids droop and Morpheus nears.

'Twould be the best confession I could make—
   For you would blot out memories of my past
   Mistakes, and give your love to me, perhaps, at last,
And I'd grow deeper, broader, fuller for your sake.
Clarence W. Kip.

There is no degree in loving; you must give all or none.

VERSE & WORSE

MY WISH.

Would that I had some subtle power
   To ken thy mind unknown to thee,
To live thy life in spirit daily—
   To guide thy heart, so dear to me.
Clarence W. Kip.

Fate may deny me love, but not loving. The honor of it is not yours, but mine—I am proud that I am man enough to love you.

You are not to blame if I care for you, nor am I, perhaps—but that unmerciful thing that people call Fate, or Providence, or God.

VERSE & WORSE

QUITE ENOUGH.

You wanted my love, and you took it,
    For what are your victims to do?
You're not sweet sixteen, tho' you look it,
    And hearts are but trifles to you.
You gained a delightful sensation
    When I pleased you by bending the knee,
You rose in your own estimation—
    You wanted my love, but not me.
Selected.

Every time a button drops off it puts more responsibility on the others.

Beauty provoketh thieves sooner than gold.

VERSE & WORSE

FOUR FEET ON A FENDER.

It is anthracite coal, and the fender is low,
    Steel barred is the grate—and the tiles
Handpainted in figures:—the one at the top
    Is a Japanese lady who smiles.
There's an ormolu clock on the mantel; above
    Is a masterpiece: facit Gerome;
On the fender four feet—my young wife's
      feet and mine
    Trimly shod, in a row and, at home.

My slippers are broidered of velvet and silk—
    The work of her fingers before
We stood at the altar. To have them made
      up
    Cost me just a round five dollars more
Than a new pair had cost at my bootmaker's
      shop;
    But each stitch was a token of love,
And she shall never know. Ah, how easy
      they are
    On their perch the steel fender above.

VERSE & WORSE

FOUR FEET ON A FENDER—Continued.

Words fail me to tell of her own. There's
  a chest
 In her grandfather's garret, and there
'Mid a thousand strange things of a century
  past,
 She discovered this ravishing pair.
They are small, trim and natty; their color is
  red,
 And each have the funniest heel.
White balbrigan stockings, high-clocked, underneath,
 These décolleté slippers reveal.

Ah, many a time in my grandfather's day
 They led the old fellow a dance;
They were bought with Virginia tobacco,
  and came—
 Who would guess it? Imported from
  France.
How odd that yon stern-faced ancestor of
  mine,
 In the earlier days of his life,
Should have loved her who tripped in these
  red slippers then—
 The young grandmamma of my wife.

VERSE & WORSE

FOUR FEET ON A FENDER—Continued.

The course of some true loves, at least runs
    not smooth;
  And I'm glad that 'tis so when I see
The trim, dainty feet in the red slippers there,
  Which belong to my lady—and me!
Two short months ago in this snug little room
  I sat in this soft cushioned seat;
No companion was near save my pipe. Now
    behold
  On the polished steel fender four feet.

Let them prate of the happiness Paradise
    yields
  To the Moslem—the raptures that thrill
The soul of the Hindu whom Juggernaut
    takes—
  The bless of Gan-Eden; and still
I believe that no gladness that man has con-
    ceived
  Can compare with the tranquilized state
That springs from two small feet alongside
    one's own,
  On the fender in front of his grate.

VERSE & WORSE

FOUR FEET ON A FENDER—Continued.

In vain the illusion. The trim feet are gone,
    They pass by my door every day—
Yet they stop not nor tarry, but swiftly pass on—
    Nor can I persuade them to stay.
And a bachelor's dreams are but dreams at the best,
    Be they ever so fond or so sweet.
The anthracite blaze has burned low, and behold
    On the fender two lonesome old feet.
                      Anonymous.

Men do stop serving the Devil long enough to sleep; but women lose no such time—they go on dreaming up some new plan of contrariness.